The hills that built me

The hills that built me

SEGAPELO BOOKS

Samuel Kagiso Segapelo

Cover designed by: Segapelo IT Solutions
Published by: Segapelo Books
www.segapelobooks.co.za

Thank you for purchasing "The hills that built me". Please feel free to share your thoughts with me and others.
Email: segapelosamuel@gmail.com

The hills that built me,
Anthology of life inspiring poems

Acknowlegements

Writing this book has been an incredible journey, and it would not have been possible without the support and inspiration of so many wonderful people.

First and foremost, I would like to express my deepest gratitude to my family, as they have always been my rock and my source of strength. Their unwavering love and support have sustained me through the ups and downs of this project, and I am forever grateful for their encouragement and believing in me.

Finally, I want to express my gratitude to the readers who have picked up this book. Your interest and support are truly humbling, and I hope that this book inspires and motivates you as much as it has inspired me.

Thank you all for being a part of this journey.

Contents

Strive for greatness 1

Towards a destination 2

Wake up with a positive mind...3

The unseen beauty...4

A heart so rich 6

Lost opportunity..8

My passion..10

My fear drove me down..11

I can't let go of anger 12

Should I forgive? 13

My anger keeps me alive..14

Who am I? 16

Cherish them while you still can 17

Essence of love 18

I am Innocent..19

The hills that built me..20

Trust in yourself...21

There is treasure in every idea 22

Hard way to success 23

I wasted my life 24

Your time will come...26

Healing after losing a loved one 27

Am I alone 28

I found Myself..29

Be humble...30

All he wants is respect 31

Art is beauty 32

What a great achievement 33

I stand alone...34

Imaginary friend 35

Lost hope 36

I have survived..37

Tough road 38

Manner, the best gift 39

A woman with strength 40

Born to rule...42

As we hustle 43

Shuttered dreams...44

I am unique 46

I am the ghost of the street..47

Little baby born...48

When duty calls...49

Accept my apology 50

I choose to be happy 51

It all changed in a second...52

long illness 53

Have I sold my soul? 54

Stress and depression 55

A father, a hero..56

Mother's love..57

Accept me as I am...58

Strength of a family...59

I am Youth, I have more to Conquer 60

Live to understand your destiny 61

Where are we heading? 62

Dear student..63

Reclaim your life..64

Don't bottle up, open up..65

Life is a blessing 66

Celebrate yourself 68

All I have is happiness..69

You are far away 70

Peace and healing as I travel...71

Sharing is caring..72

Growing up comes with a responsibility........................73

So much pain...74

It was mine and I let it go...75

Simplify your life...76

When the Dream is over 77

I will shower you with love 78

The future is in our hands 79

Self-Esteem 80

Your mind is your weapon 81

I hold this pen in my hand, writing poems..................82

I. 82

II. 83

About the Author 84

About the book 85

In life, we all need motivation and inspiration to overcome the challenges we face. We need to find the strength to lift ourselves up when we fall and keep moving forward when the road gets tough, and never lose focus on our goals and dreams.

Strive for greatness

Push yourself every day,
In every single way,
Challenge your limits,
And reach new heights.

Don't settle for less,
Strive for greatness passionately,
Embrace the struggle,
And face your fears bravely.

You have great potential,
So don't let it go to waste,
Unlock your inner strength,
And enlighten your day.

Rise up to the challenge,
And refuse to be held back,
Let perseverance and determination,
Be your guiding lights along your way.

Push yourself every day,
With unwavering commitment,
And watch as you grow,
And achieve your ultimate fulfillment.

Towards a destination

Towards a destination yet unknown,
We travel on this road we've sown,
With hope and faith to guide our way,
Through the unknown twists and sway.

Sometimes the path is straight and clear,
Other times, we're consumed by fear,
But we keep moving, step by step,
Towards the horizon, with no regrets.

The journey takes us far and wide,
Through mountains tall and rivers wide,
With each step, a lesson learned,
And with each turn, a new page turned.

We may stumble, we may fall,
But we rise up, standing tall,
For we know the journey's end,
Will bring us to our hearts' content.

So towards a destination yet untold,
We keep moving, bold and bold,
For life's adventure is the ride,
And our destination is the wave journey.

Wake up with a positive mind

Wake up with a smile on your face,
Embrace the new day with grace.
Leave yesterday's worries behind,
Focus on the good in your mind.

Take a deep breath and feel the air,
Let go of any stress or despair.
Think of all the possibilities,
Opportunities and probabilities.

Start your day with a positive thought,
Let it guide you through any knots.
See the beauty in the world around,
And let the happiness overflow.

Choose kindness, love and compassion,
That's the only way to true satisfaction.
Wake up with a heart full of joy,
And let the day be your toy.

Believe in yourself and your dreams,
And nothing is as impossible as it seems.
Wake up with a positive vibe,
And conquer the day with your loved ones.

The unseen beauty

The world may seem wild and unclear,
But in the middle of the noise, beauty is always near,
It whispers in the breeze, and hums in the air,
A reminder of the wonder we often overlook.

It is in the blooming of a flower in the field,
In the warmth of the sun that gently yields,
In the vibrant colors of the setting sun,
In the peaceful quiet when the day is done.

The unseen beauty is in the kindness we show,
In the gentle touch that helps us to grow,
In the love we give and the love we receive,
In the connections we make that help us believe.

It's in the strength of a heart that's been broken,
In the perseverance that leaves us awoken,
In the resilience that guides us through,
In the moments that make us feel anew.

So let us look beyond the chaos of the day,
And seek the unseen beauty that is here to stay,
For it's a reminder of all that's right,
And a source of hope to shine so bright.

And though it may be hard to see at times,
The unseen beauty is always there, waiting to sound,
A reminder that amidst the chaos and strife,
There's a world of wonder that's full of life.

A heart so rich

A heart so rich with love to give,
overflowing with empathy and grace.
A soul so kind, so warm and true,
embracing all with an open heart.

It beats a rhythm that soothes the soul,
a melody that beat deep within.
A heart so rich with tenderness,
that hurts and fears cannot help but give in.

It whispers words that heal the hurt,
a balm that heals and comforts the pain.
A heart so rich with compassion,
that understanding and love always reign.

It showers blessings on those in need,
giving freely without any thought of gain.
A heart so rich with generosity,
that it truly believes in sharing the gain.

It forgives all the wrongs that happen,
and lets go of hurts that had once been.
A heart so rich with forgiveness,
that it moves forward and leaves the past unseen.

A heart so rich with beauty and light,
that it light up each and every day.
If only all could have such a heart,
then surely this world would be a greater place to stay.

Lost opportunity

A chance once given that I let slip away,
Like sand that slips between my fingers.
A moving moment, a moment lost,
Was all it took for my dreams to be lost.

I knew the risks, the fear, the doubts,
But I never took the chance to shout out,
My heart's desire, to let it all out,
 And now I'm left with nothing but a silent shout.

The opportunity was like a bird in flight,
That moved smoothly through the sky with great delight,
 But I hesitated and chose not to fight,
The fear inside me, it held me tight.

Regret and sorrow now fill my soul,
 For the lost opportunity has taken its way,
The door that once opened now forever closed,
And I am left with a frozen heart.

Oh, how I wish I could turn back time,
To the day of the lost opportunity, to make it mine,
To grab the moment, to make it shine,
But sadly, it's gone, forever confined.

So, let this be a lesson, to all who seek,
To grab a chance, to be brave and dive,
For nothing is won by the weak and meek,
Only by those who dare to dream and never sleep.

My passion

My passion is a flame that burns bright,
A fire that never dims in sight,
 It drives me on through every day,
And helps me find my own way.

It keeps me warm when life is cold,
And gives me strength when I feel old,
It fuels my dreams and lights my path,
And gives me hope in bad times.

My passion is what sets me free,
And makes me, who I want to be,
It gives me wings to fly so high,
And helps me reach the sky.

It's what I live for every day,
And what I'll never let slip away,
For my passion is what gives me life,
And fills me up with endless strength.

So here's to the flame that never dies,
And to the fire that fills the skies,
My passion will always burn so bright,
And guide me on towards the light.

My fear drove me down

My fear drove me down,
Deep into the ground,
As I struggled and fought,
But sadness wasn't found.

I tried to break free,
But fear held its key,
Limiting my thoughts,
And draining my hopes.

I lost my way,
In the darkness of disappointment,
 As fear consumed me,
And everything I could see.

But then I gained some strength,
And I fought back at length,
Against the fear that held me,
And stopped me from being free.

I found my light,
In the darkest of the night,
And fear slowly drifted away,
As my mind danced and played.

Now with my head held high,
And joy in my eyes, I take a step forward,
As fear fades into the background.

I can't let go of anger

I can't let go of my anger,
It clings to me like a vice.
A burning fire that never fades,
I hold on tight, paying the price.

Every slight, every wrong,
Echoes in my mind each day.
I am consumed by my fury,
And don't know how to break away.

The world seems so unfair,
I feel wronged at every turn.
I can't let go of my anger,
My heart will always break.

I know that it's not healthy,
To hold on to the bitter thoughts.
But I can't release the anger,
I feel it's all I've got.

I hope one day I'll find peace,
And let go of all this rage.
But until that day arrives,
I'm trapped in this dark cage.

I can't let go of my anger,
It's become a part of me.
But I'll keep fighting to be free,
And finally find my harmony.

Should I forgive?

That is the question, when I've been hurt,
Should I let go of the tension?
It's not easy, to let bygones be bygones,
To ignore the pain and to move on.

But what's the alternative, holding on grudges?
 To let anger and bitterness slowly eat away at my heart's
hedges?
No, it's better to forgive, to let the healing begin,
To find peace in the situation and let go of the sin.

It doesn't mean I forget, or that what was done was okay,
It just means that I choose to let love pave the way.
To find understanding and empathy,
To release myself from the burden of what's not right.

So, should I forgive? Yes, I believe it's true,
For in forgiveness lies the power to renew.
To find a new beginning, a chance to start afresh,
 And to live with purpose and joy,
Free from the past's distress.

My anger keeps me alive

My anger keeps me alive.
A fire within my soul
Eagerness to fight
A will to take control.

It fuels my every step
A passion never extinguishes,
A force that I have kept,
Though often it's not at rest.

It roars and it rages
An unstoppable force
A storm that never ages
A tempest with no remorse.

My anger keeps me alive.
It's both a strength and curse
 A power that I must thrive
But also must traverse

For though it gives me power
It can also bring me down
And I must never cower
But learn to wear its crown.

So I'll harness this emotion
And deal it with intent
A force of pure devotion
That cannot be bent.

For my anger keeps me alive
And I will let it burn
A flame that will survive
And never will it turn.

Who am I?

Who am I? That simple question,
Seeking to know my own identity,
A complex puzzle, a mystery,
Waiting to be solved, so eagerly.

Am I the product of my experiences,
The product of my upbringing,
Or am I defined by my choices, my chances,
And the paths I am now travel.

Am I my name, my profession,
My heritage or my beliefs,
Or the sum of all my passion,
And the journey that my heart seeks.

I am the smile that spreads my face,
When I help someone in need,
The tears that stain my cheeks,
When I feel the weight of grief.

I am the laughter that fills my soul,
When surrounded by those I love,
The voice that speaks my truth,
And the courage to rise above.

I am me, defined by all and none,
A unique masterpiece, one of a kind,
With strengths and flaws, that makes me human,
And a spirit that's free, and unconfined.

Cherish them while you still can

Cherish them while you still can
These moments with your loved ones
For time moves too quickly
And memories are all that remain.

Hold them close in your heart
Those precious laughs and smiles
For life is but a fleeting moment
And tomorrow is never guaranteed.

Take the time to truly connect
Hug them a little tighter
Show them how much they mean to you
And create memories to last a lifetime.

For one day they may no longer be there
And you'll long for just one more moment
To tell them how much you love them
And cherish them once more, while you still can.

Essence of love

Love is the beating heart within,
An endless flame that cannot dim.
It shines on through life's darkest nights,
And fill our souls with pure delight.

It is warm like a gentle breeze,
That rustles through the tallest trees.
It never fades, it never dies,
It always shines bright in our eyes.

It whispers softly in our ears,
And guide us through each time.
It makes us whole, it makes us kind,
It fill our hearts and free our minds.

For love is not just a mere emotion,
It is a connection, a devotion.
It is the essence of all that is right,
It's what gives meaning to our life.

So hold it tight, don't let it go,
Let your love shine and let it grow.
For love is the greatest gift of all,
The essence of life, that we recall.

I am Innocent

I am but a mere soul,
Filled with pure innocence and love.
My heart, untouched by any evil,
Guided only by the stars above.

I have done no harm to anyone,
My hands are clean of any guilt.
My path is of kindness and compassion,
A path that I will forever build.

No crime has ever been committed,
No wrong has ever been done.
I am a humble servant,
A faithful child of the sun.

My heart is open, my intentions are clear,
My eyes sparkle with gentle light.
I am innocent, I am pure,
A soul so free and bright.

The hills that built me

The hills that built me were strong and true,
Guiding me forward when I didn't know what to do.
They stood tall and firm,
Teaching me to be brave and tough.

Through rocky grounds and stormy weather,
Their continuous support kept me together.
They listened to my sorrows and joys,
And taught me to rise above life's expectation.

Each hill had a story to tell,
Of victories, struggles, and battles fought well.
They paved the way for a brighter tomorrow,
Helping me to get rid my unhappiness.

As I stand tall and face life's test,
I lean on the hills that gave me their best.
I am grateful to these strong pillars of love,
Who raised me up with strength from above.

So here's to the hills that built me,
Each one is a treasure that I'll forever see.
Their love and spirit will always live on,
For the hills that built me, I will always cherish.

Trust in yourself

In this journey of life,
There will be moments of doubt,
Uncertainty and fear,
But don't let them knock you out.

Trust in yourself,
And believe in your worth,
You have the strength within,
To conquer this earth.

Don't let anyone tell you,
What you can or cannot do,
Your path is yours to create,
And your dreams are yours to pursue.

Listen to your heart,
And follow your instinct,
Only you know what's best,
For your own ambition.

Have faith in yourself,
And take that leap of faith,
You'll be surprised at how far,
Your own courage can take.

So go ahead, take the force,
And take charge of your life,
Trust in yourself, my dear,
And you will surely flourish.

There is treasure in every idea

There is treasure in every idea,
A gem waiting to be found,
But be careful who you present it to,

Some people may not see the worth,
Of what you have to say,
And they may bury it beneath the dirt,
Where it will never see the light of day.

But others may see the potential,
And help it grow and shine,
They will nourish and encourage,
And make it something divine.

So be careful who you share with,
Choose wisely who you confide,
For there is treasure in every idea,
And it deserves a chance to thrive.

Hard way to success

The journey we take to reach success,
Is full of trials and tests.
It's a winding road, steep and long,
At times it may feel like everything's gone wrong.

But those who hold on and never give in,
Are the ones who ultimately win.
For every setback, every defeat,
Is a chance to learn, grow.

Though the journey may be tough and hard,
It's the struggle that shapes us, makes us strong.
We learn to be resilient, wise, and brave,
To see the world through different eyes.

We come to know that failure's not the end,
But a chance to start again, to make amends.
We understand that success is not just a prize,
But a state of being, a mindset, that we must realize.

So if you are on the road to success,
And feeling lost, discouraged, or stressed,
Remember that the hard way is the best,
For it challenges us and puts us to the test.

Keep pushing forward, keep striving on,
And soon enough, your battles will be won.
For success is not just about the end,
But the journey itself, and the lessons learned.

I wasted my life

I wasted my life, I truly did,
Time slipped away like a forgotten lid,
Days turned into years, years into decades,
And yet, my dreams were never renovated.

I chased after what society considered success,
But in doing so, I created unending stress,
Money, fame, and power were my goals,
But they left me feeling empty and alone.

I didn't make time for my loved ones,
I missed out on life's joyful moments,
And when I finally realized my mistakes,
It was too late, and my heart began to ache.

Regret overwhelmed me, like a dark, suffocating cloud,
I wished I could turn back time, but there was no way
I wasted the precious gift of life,
And I was left to stand the burden of my challenge.

So, to all my fellow beings,
To learn from me and never delay,
Chase your passions,
Cherish your moments and never let them slip away,
Focus on love, kindness, and the simple things,
For they are the treasures that life truly bring.

Focus on yourself

Focus on yourself,
and the things that make you whole.
Discover all the treasures,
that live within your soul.

Embrace your unique qualities,
and let your true self shine.
Celebrate your accomplishments,
and learn from each decline.

Take time to reflect,
and find your inner peace.
Listen to your heart's desires,
and let them never die.

look after your mind and body,
with love and self-care,
that you deserve and worth,
of all the joy and care.

Remember, you are enough,
just as you are today.
Keep evolving and growing,
and you will find your way.

So focus on yourself,
and let your light shine bright.
For when you are whole,
you will live an happy life.

Your time will come

Your time will come, dear one,
No need to rush,
Life will unfold in its own way,
Just trust the journey, that comes your way.

Do not fear the unknown,
Embrace it as your own,
For it holds beauty and light,
That will guide you through the night.

Patience is the key,
The road may twist and bend,
But every step you take,
Will bring you closer to your fate.

You have a purpose, a plan,
A destiny that is all yours,
So walk with grace,
And let your true self be shown.

Your time will come, I promise,
And when it does, you'll know,
For the stars will align,
And your heart will truly glow.

So never give up, my dear,
Stay strong and genuine,
For your time is just around the bend,
And it's bound to be magnificent.

Healing after losing a loved one

The pain of loss seeps deep within,
A heart once whole, now broken and thin,
The ache inside felt every day,
Our loved one now so far away.

The tears we shed, the words we speak,
The memories we hold, so priceless and neat,
We smile and laugh, but deep inside,
The pain persists, we cannot hide.

Yet healing comes, so softly at first,
A glimmer of hope, a gentle burst,
The love we shared, so strong and true,
A guiding light to help us through.

With time, the pain will slowly fade,
But the love we had will never end,
Forever in our hearts, our loved one shall stay,
A precious gift we shall cherish each day.

So though we grieve, we must embrace,
The hope that shines with each new day,
For healing comes as we let go,
Allowing peace and love to flow.

Am I alone

Am I alone in my thoughts and my fears?
No one seems to listen or hear,
The words that spill from my lips.
They fall on deaf ears, like forgotten ships.

Do I find the way in this world on my own?
With no one to talk to, no place to call home.
My heart aches with a feeling so true.
No one seems to see the essence of me,
I'm not even on their action plans.

Silence fills the air around me
My thoughts strong like a wild sea
No one seems to understand
What it's like to be alone in a crowded land

But wait, there's a light of hope
Maybe I'm not alone, somehow I cope
For there is a presence within me
A voice that reminds me I am free.

Free to be who I am, unique and true
Free to explore the world with a different view
No longer do I need affirmation
For I am me, and that's my greatest desire.

I found Myself

In the middle of confusion,
Lost and searching for my own conclusion,
Wondering who I am and where I belong,
Lost in the crowd and feeling so alone.

But then I took a moment to breathe,
To look within and try to believe,
That within me lies the power and strength,
To be who I am and go to the great length.

I found myself in the simplest things,
In the way the sunlight dances and sings,
In the gentle touch of the morning breeze,
In the laughter of a child's playful tease.

I found myself in the love I give,
In the kindness I share and the way I live,
In the dreams I have and the goals I pursue,
In every step that I take, every path that I choose.

And now I am no longer lost or unsure,
I am confident, strong, and fully mature,
For I have found myself in the beauty of life,
And I know I can overcome any difficulty.

Be humble

Be humble in all that you do,
For arrogance will not see you through.
Remember that we're all the same,
No matter the wealth or fame.

Treat others with kindness and respect,
And always give a helping hand when you can.
There is someone who needs it, someone in pain,
And in this way, you'll never be in worthless.

Don't think too highly of yourself,
For we're all easily broken and in need of help.
Accept your mistakes, and work to improve,
And to your character, you'll always be true.

So be humble, my dear friend,
For a heart that is proud will always offend.
But with humbleness as your guide,
You'll go far and wide.

All he wants is respect

All he wants is respect,
For the battles he fights each day,
For the obstacles he overcomes,
On his journey along the way.

He long to be acknowledged,
For his hard work and sacrifice,
For the time and effort he puts in,
To make his life and others' nice.

He craves for recognition,
For the struggles he has faced,
For the strength and determination,
He has shown in his race.

He desires to be appreciated,
For the love that he gives,
For the kindness and compassion,
That he chooses to live.

All he wants is respect,
For the person that he is,
For the qualities and virtues,
That make him one of a kind, and bliss.

So listen when he speaks,
And understand his point of view,
Give him the respect he deserves,
And watch his spirit renew.

Art is beauty

Art is beauty, in every form and shape,
A creation that the heart and soul both make,
A masterpiece, a vision that's sublime,
A reflection of the artist in time.

From brushstrokes on canvas to words on a page,
Art can evoke emotions and captivate,
A symphony that fills the air with sound,
Or a sculpture that leaves one spellbound.

The colors blend and dance in harmony,
As the artist pours out their heart and energy,
Creating something unique, profound,
A treasure to be shared and passed around.

Art speaks to the heart in a language pure,
A message that has the power to endure,
To inspire, to heal, to move and console,
Art is beauty, the essence of the soul.

What a great achievement

What a great achievement,
To climb the highest peak,
To conquer every challenge,
And never grow weak.

To reach for the stars,
And touch them with your hands,
To push through the pain,
And never lose your stand.

To strive for excellence,
In everything you do,
To never settle for less,
And always see it through.

What a great achievement,
To leave a lasting mark,
To inspire others to follow,
And light up the dark.

To leave behind a legacy,
That will never fade away,
To always be remembered,
And shine like a star each day.

So keep on pushing forward,
And always reach for more,
For what a great achievement,
To truly rise.

I stand alone

I stand alone with my thoughts and fears
Facing my truth, my doubts, my tears
The weight of the world on my shoulders
As I find a way through life's possibilites.

I stand alone with my dreams and
Goals pushing forward, reaching for my soul's
Desires, passions, and ambitions,
Striving for success and recognition.

I stand alone with my strengths and flaws
Embracing all, never hiding from the truth
The good and bad are parts of me
And I accept them both, happily.

So I stand alone, but not apart,
With an open mind and kind heart
Ready to face whatever comes my way
And make the most of every single day.

Imaginary friend

Invisible to everyone but me,
My imaginary friend.
We laugh and play each passing day,
Endlessly, happy all the time .

You may not see the joy we share,
Or the games we play without a care.
But I know that you are always near,
To give a listening ear.

In times of victory and in the sad,
You are the only friend I've ever had.
You never judge or criticize,
And your love never dies.

Though some may mock and call you fake,
I know the bond we share won't break.
For in this world, where love is scarce,
You're the one who's always there.

So here's to you, my imaginary friend,
A bond that never seems to end.
May we continue to laugh and play,
As we journey on, day by day.

Lost hope

When you feel like hope is gone,
And the road ahead seems so long,
Remember that you are strong,
And you can rise above the wrong.

Though the clouds may block your view,
And the world may seem out of line,
Hold on to what you know is true,
And let your heart guide you through.

For every storm will pass,
And the sun will shine at last,
Just have faith and hope will redefine,
A brighter future, better than any.

So don't give up or lose faith,
For life will bring a change of pace,
And within you lies the strength and grace,
To overcome any obstacle you face.

I have survived

I have survived,
All the embarrassment,
Humiliation, and pain,
That life has thrown my way.

I have held my head high,
Even when I wanted to crawl into a hole.
I have picked myself up,
Even when I felt like I couldn't carry on.

I have learned to laugh,
Even when everything seems hopeless.
I have found my inner strength,
When I thought I had nothing to find.

Through the heartache and sorrow,
I have found my way out.
I have faced my fears,
and moved over my doubt.

So now I stand tall,
Proud of all I have become.
I have survived,
And I know I'm not done.

Tough road

When the road is rough and long,
And it feels like giving up is strong,
Remember that within you lies,
A fire that never really dies.

When the weight of the world is too much,
And everything seems out of touch,
Remember that you are stronger than you know,
And your spirit will never let you go.

For the battle may be hard and challenging,
But you have the courage to step up,
And with each step you take you'll find,
That the power within will never die.

So don't give up, don't ever quit,
For within you lies the courage to carry on,
And in the end, when you reach the top,
You'll know you never gave up, and that's a lot.

Manner, the best gift

From a tender age they taught me how to act,
To say please and thank you, to show respect.

"Not with your mouth full" my mother would teach,
I learned to chew quietly and keep my chin high.

"Cover your mouth when you sneeze or cough",
My father would remind me, his voice always soft.

I said "yes sir" and "no ma'am", always polite,
Holding doors and saying sorry when it's right.

They said it was important, these manners we had,
To show that we're kind, and not bitter or mad.

As I grew older, I didn't forget,
All the lessons I learned, from them I'd never regret.

It's become a part of me, my manners and grace,
I try to be kind, to show others my face.

And as I look back, with a heart full of thanks,
I bless them for guiding me in these righteous path.

For being raised with manners was the best gift,
It's given me kindness, and a spirit that's pure and uplifted!

A woman with strength

She stands tall and proud,
With a heart full of grace,
A woman with strength,
Who knows her rightful place.

She doesn't shy away,
From a path that's tough,
She faces all challenges,
Knowing she's more than enough.

She bears life's burdens,
With a smile on her face,
A woman with strength,
Who makes the world a better place.

She rises from hard times,
With a heart full of fire,
A woman with strength,
Who'll never grow weaker.

She lives life on her terms,
With her head held high,
A woman with strength,
Who'll always try.

Her presence fills the room,
With a warmth and light,
A woman with strength,
Who shines so bright.

So let us celebrate,
This woman strong and true,
For the world needs her,
And all that she can do.

Born to rule

We all have unique paths to tread,
And destinies to fulfill ahead
From our very first breath,
Our purpose awaits, not just for death.

We each have strengths and flaws,
And unique talents that give us cause
To inspire and lead in our own way,
With kindness and compassion every day.

We're not just born to rule,
But to serve and help, to be a tool
For the betterment of humankind,
To leave the world a better find.

Our reign is not about absolute power,
But about using our gifts to empower others
To be their best selves too,
And make a positive impact through and through.

Obstacles and challenges will come,
But with perseverance, we can overcome
And inspire others to do the same,
To grow and evolve, and create a better game.

Born to lead, but also to serve,
Our purpose is to help and preserve
The world for future generations to come,
And leave a legacy of love and wisdom.

As we hustle

As we hustle through the day,
Trying to find our way,
We strive towards our goal,
And let nothing lifeless our soul.

The world can be so loud,
And sometimes we feel so small,
But deep within, we all know,
We have the strength to stand tall.

Through the struggles,
We keep pushing on in life,
We exercise our will and great power,
To make our dreams fly high.

With the power of our mind,
And the freedom to unwind,
We conquer every obstacle,
And find success that is unstoppable.

So let's keep moving forward,
And never let our dreams fail,
For with the passion in our heart,
We can all become the Writers.

Of a stories worth telling,
With a life that is worth living,
As we hustle towards our goal,
And keep on going up.

Shuttered dreams

My dreams are locked away,
Like they're hidden in a corner.
I used to feel hopeful, but now it's all gone,
It's like I'm stuck in the shadows, and can't move on.

I want to chase my dreams, to reach up high,
To make them real, and let them fly.
But fear and doubt holding me down,
It's like I'm trapped in a cage, and can't be found.

I try to protect myself, with walls built high,
But all they do is keep me confined.
My heart is screaming, for a chance to break free,
To let my dreams fly high and be mine.

And then a light of hope starts to shine,
A little spark, that becomes a sign.
A voice whispers, "don't be afraid",
It's time to break free, and find your own way.

So I reach out, and take hold of the key,
To unlock my dreams, and set them free.
I face my fears, with a fire in my heart,
And take the first step, to a brand new beginning.

The doors to my dreams are wide open now,
As I step outside, and take my first bow.
I spread my wings, and take up to the sky,
I'm dancing with life full of joy.

My dreams are no longer shuttered away,
For I've found the courage.
I'm following my heart, to a joyful tune,
And chasing my dreams, all the way to the moon.

I am unique

I feel like I'm one of a kind,
No one else can replicate my mind.
My voice, my thoughts, my ideas, my style,
They all come together, to make me worthwhile.

I'm not perfect; I have my mistakes and weakness,
But that's what makes me special.
I never hide who I am, ,
I'm real, it's who I am and who I'll always be.

My talents, my skills, my passions and desires,
All set me apart, they fuel my inner fires.
I embrace my identity, my individuality shines bright,
I'm unique, and that's something to celebrate.

I don't want to blend in, I want to stand out,
My reality is what I'm all about.
I'm proud of who I am, and what I can do,
I'm unique, and that's delightful.

I am the ghost of the street

I am the ghost of the street,
Silent witness to life on the beat,
I move among the crowds,
But nobody hears my sound.

I have no home, no place to stay,
No shelter from the night or day,
I roam from street to street,
A lonely soul with weary feet.

I watch the people as they pass,
Their laughter and joy beyond my grasp,
I wonder what it's like to feel,
The warmth of love that's truly real.

The memories haunt me every day,
Of family and friends who've gone away,
I am but a shadow of my past,
A lost soul in a transient cast.

So, I wander on, alone and free,
A ghost that no one else can see,
A reminder of what lies ahead,
For those who have no home or bed.

Little baby born

Little baby born, so tiny and so new,
With chubby cheeks and eyes so bright.
You've come into this world with a little cry,
And brought so much joy to those nearby.

Your tiny hands and feet are such a sight,
And your smile so pure and full of light.
You've brightened up our day with your presence,
A precious gift of pure innocence.

We'll watch you grow and learn every day,
And be there for you in every way.
Little baby born, so full of hope and possibility,
May your life be filled with love and peace.

When duty calls

When duty calls, we must all stand tall,
And answer with courage, one and all.
Our country, our people, need us to be strong,
To fight for what's right, to battle for long.

We leave our families, our homes behind,
And travel to places where danger we'll find.
We do what we must, to keep others safe,
To protect and defend, with firm grace.

Our hearts may be heavy, our spirits so low,
But one thing we know, that we have to go.
For the job is ours, it's our dedicated vow,
To serve and protect, to fight for now.

We stand brave and bold, with pride in our hearts,
Ready for battle, ready to do our part.
For we are heroes, in every sense of the word,
Our courage will always be heard.

So when duty calls, we'll rise to the task,
We'll fight with courage, we'll never ask.
For we have a mission, and we'll see it through,
For our country, our people, for me and you.

Accept my apology

I write this poem to express my deepest regret,
For any hurt or harm that I may have caused you yet,
I'm sorry for the words I spoke without thinking,
And for any actions that were hurtful.

Please accept my apology with an open heart,
I wish to make amends and make a brand new start,
For I value your friendship and cherish your trust,
And I know my behavior has caused you quite a fuss.

I promise to listen more and think before I speak,
To be more considerate and less quick to critique,
I'll do my best to show you that I've learned my lesson,
And that my apology is sincere without question.

Please don't hold my mistake against me forever,
Let's move on from this and start over our friendship,
I hope you can forgive me and accept my apology,
So we can continue our journey together.

I choose to be happy

I choose to be happy, it's my choice to make,
To let go of negativity, and all that is fake.
I'll focus on the good, and what makes me smile,
And find joy in every moment.

Life can be tough, and throw us all around,
But I'll keep on going, and stand my ground.
I'll find reasons to be grateful, and give thanks each day,
And seek out inspiration, to light my way.

I refuse to let fear, or doubt hold me back,
I'll seize every opportunity, and stay on track.
I'll surround myself with love, and positive vibes,
And commit to being happy, for the rest of my life.

So here's to choosing happiness, and living life with joy.
For when we focus on the good, our minds and hearts are free,
And though there may be bumps, that come along the way.
I'll choose to be happy, and make the most of today.

It all changed in a second

In the blink of an eye, it all changed,
A moment that forever will be engraved.
Life was once filled with laughter and light,
But now darkness has taken over the night.

A tragedy struck and left us stunned,
Forced to face a new reality that had begun.
The joy we once knew was now hard to find
And sorrow and pain had become all-inclusive

The future we envisioned now uncertain and past
The hopes we held tightly had been taken away
But through helplessness and suffering
We found the strength to carry on and repair

Life may not be what we expected it to be
But we can still find happiness and stand tall and free
For in every second that passes by
We have the power to choose and will to survive.

long illness

A long illness, a heavy burden to bear
Days stretch into weeks, weeks into months
Endless doctor visits, treatments without care
Life spirals out of control, a constant hunt

For relief, for healing, for a cure
Hope fluctuates, sometimes soars sometimes dies
Family and friends come through, strong and pure
Words of encouragement, love, and cries

The body weakens, the mind takes a toll
Isolation and pain become the norm
The road seems endless, and the end of goal
unable to be understood, just a distant storm

Yet in the middle of darkness, there's a light
Faith and prayers, a source of renewal
A silver lining, a relief in sight
A promise of healing, a hope for renewal

As the body fights to recover and heal
Days begin to brighten, hope takes hold
Strength returns, the heart starts to feel
Gratitude and joy begin to unfold

The long illness is now a memory, a scar
But it reminds us of the value of life
A reminder to cherish each moment, no matter how far
And to always have hope, through pain and strife.

Have I sold my soul?

Have I sold my soul for silver and gold,
For power and wealth that I can hold?
Have I let greed consume my heart,
And torn my soul and spirit apart?

Have I forgotten the things that matter,
Forgetting love and joy, becoming sadder?
Have I ignored the beauty of life,
Turning away from peace and ending in trouble?

The price I paid, was it worth it all?
This emptiness inside, can I stop the fall?
Can I reclaim the goodness in me,
And restore the lost harmony?

For if I have sold my soul and lost my way,
Let me turn back and find light each day.
Let me live with honor and love,
And find my true worth above.

Stress and depression

Stress and depression, a never-ending wave,
a dangerous force that just won't fall.
The weight on your chest, the ache in your heart,
A constant reminder that you're falling apart.

The world seems suffocating, a heavy veil,
It feels like there's no way out of this cloud.
Every day is a battle, a war with your mind,
A struggle to leave all your worries behind.

The darkness surrounds you, it's hard to escape,
And the more that you try, the more you feel trapped.
You long for a spark of hope to break through,
To show you a path that you can pursue.

But all that you feel is that endless loss of hope,
A sense of helplessness you can't help but share.
The weight of the world feels too much to bear,
As you wonder how anyone could ever care.

Yet in the middle of all this overwhelming difficulty,
You'll find the strength to pull through this life.
With a little bit of help, and a lot of self-care,
You'll find a way to breathe in the fresh air.

So keep pushing and fighting, despite how tough it may seem,
For no one can steal away your dreams.
You've got this, believe in yourself, hold on tight,
For every ending brings a new daylight.

A father, a hero

A father, a hero, strong and true,
Through thick and thin, he sees us through.
A guiding light, a shining star,
He shows us all, no matter how far.

A listening ear, a helping hand,
He's always there to understand.
He teaches us to stand up tall,
To never give up, to give our all.

His heart is pure, his love is deep,
He comforts us when we shed tears.
No matter what life throws at our way,
He always knows just what to say.

With every step, with every breath,
He leads us on the path of success.
And though we may grow,
His lessons guide us day by day.

So here's to fathers, our loyal friends,
Our mentors and biggest fans.
May we all strive to be like them,
And honor them until the end.

Mother's love

A mother's love is pure and true,
A love that lasts forever through.
It knows no bounds, and no limits.
A love that wipes away each tear.

Her love is gentle, kind and warm,
A love that shields from every storm.
It guides us through the darkest days,
A love that shows us better ways.

From birth until we are grown,
Her love is never fully shown.
A boundless love that's always there,
A love that shows how much she cares.

No words could ever truly say,
How much a mother's love will stay.
It's that love that we will cherish,
And remember all our days to come.

She is an angel in disguise,
Whose love and care we can't deny.
For all the times she has held our hands,
We're grateful for her love so grand.

A mother's love is priceless, pure,
A love we all can't ignore.
It's a love that will forever stay,
And guide us along life's perfect way.

Accept me as I am

Accept me as I am,
With all my flaws and quirks.
Embrace the way I move,
And all my little quirks.

My words may not be perfect,
But they come from the heart.
I may look somehow,
But I try to play the part.

I am not always sure,
Of what the future holds.
But I will always stand,
And try to be so bold.

So please do not judge me,
By the way that I look.
Look beyond the surface,
And you will see me clear.

Accept me as I am,
And I will do the same.
We'll walk together hand in hand,
In sunshine and in rain.

Strength of a family

Blood is thicker than water,
A saying we all know,
For family is a bond,
That only love can sow.

Through thick and thin we stand,
With those who share our blood,
For it's a tie that binds,
And keeps us close like mud.

We may have our differences,
And sometimes the fights may hurt,
But at the end of the day,
We're bonded by this thing.

For it's a love that's strong,
A love that never fades,
A love that's always there,
Through all the twisty shades.

So let us cherish our kin,
And hold them close each day,
For blood is thicker than water,
In every single way.

I am Youth, I have more to Conquer

I am youth, with a restless heart,
With dreams that are burning.
I am the flame that shall never part,
For I have more to conquer.

With each step, I bright a way,
And with each breath, I rise higher.
I am the melody of a fresh new day,
For I have more to conquer, I aim high.

I am fearless, and I am bold,
With an unyielding thirst for life.
I am the story yet to be told,
For I have more to conquer.

With passion in my heart, and fire in my soul,
I shall keep on, and overcome.
I am the storm, and I am whole,
For I have more to conquer, in sum.

I am youth, and I shall rise,
To the challenge of every trial.
For I am the light that never dies,
With more to conquer, and more to smile.

Live to understand your destiny

Live to understand your destiny,
Embrace the journey that lies ahead.
For though the road may seem uncertain,
It is where your path was meant to be led.

Your purpose may not be revealed,
Until you've walked a mile or two.
But trust in the guidance you're given,
And know that it will guide you through.

There may be bumps along the way,
And struggles that you must tolerate.
But keep your eyes fixed on the prize,
And let your courage help you go higher.

For in the end, it's worth the climb,
To reach the top of your heart.
Where you'll find the fulfillment you seek,
And your life's purpose will finally start.

So live to understand your destiny,
And let it be your guiding star.
For when you follow where it leads,
You'll find the purpose you're meant for.

Where are we heading?

As we hurry through life, always in a rush,
We don't often stop to think or pause.
We're moving forward, towards an unknown place,
Without knowing what we might find or face.

We strive for success, always wanting to win,
But sometimes forget what we might lose in the end.
We chase our dreams, but at what cost,
If they bring about loneliness, pain, and exhaustion.

We build towering buildings, conquer new lands,
But we must not forget nature's delicate strands.
Our actions have consequences, and we must pay heed,
To ensure a better future, for every race.

We must be mindful of the earth and its needs,
And try to protect it as we plant our seeds.
Our journey of life might lead us through trouble,
But we have the power to shape our destiny and make things
right.

We must strive for happiness, peace, and love,
And work together, hand in glove.
Let's make the world a better place,
For ourselves and future generations to embrace.

Dear student

Dear student, oh how bright you are,
With potential shining like a star.
You soak up knowledge like a sponge,
And tackle challenges with a smile.

You strive to learn and grow each day,
And push yourself in every way.
You work hard and give your best,
And take on new tasks with eagerness.

You seek out new experiences,
And learn from your mistakes and chances.
You set goals and reach for the stars,
And never let anything hold you back.

Dear student, you are an inspiration,
And a testament to dedication.
Keep shining and reaching higher,
With your passion and desire.

For you are the future, the one who will lead,
The world to greatness and make it succeed.
Keep learning, growing and shining bright,
And you'll achieve anything you set in sight.

Reclaim your life

Fetch your life, my friend,
Like a dog chasing a bone,
Run after your dreams,
Never let them alone.

Life is a treasure,
A gift that we must embrace,
Don't waste it away,
In fear or disgrace.

Find your passion,
And let it light your way,
Let nothing hold you back,
And never be led astray.

Take a great height of faith,
And fly to new heights,
Overcoming obstacles,
By using all your abilities.

Believe in yourself,
And trust in your own strength,
For only you can make,
Your life worth the length.

So reclaim your life, my friend,
hold it tight,
And don't look back,
As you journey through the night.

Don't bottle up, open up

Don't bottle up, open up,
Let your feelings flow.
For keeping them inside you,
Will only cause you great sorrow

Share your thoughts and fears,
With someone who will listen.
For holding them inside,
Can make your heart feel missing.

Reach out to a friend,
Or seek the help you need.
For talking can be healing,
And help your heart to breathe..

Don't bottle up, open up,
Let your emotions rise.
For if you keep them bottled,
They'll cause you endless cries.

Release your inner demons,
And let your feelings show.
For by opening up your heart,
You'll find the peace you've longed to know.

So don't bottle up, open up,
And let your heart be free.
For it's in sharing and connecting,
That you'll find your happiness.

Life is a blessing

Life is a blessing,
A gift from above,
A journey worth taking,
Full of wonder and love.

From the moment we're born,
To the end of our days,
We'll find ourselves learning,
In countless different ways.

We'll laugh and we'll cry,
We'll love and we'll lose,
We'll face countless challenges,
And still manage to choose.

To live every moment,
With passion and grace,
Embracing the beauty,
Of this magnificent space.

For life is a blessing,
A gift to us all,
And to live it with purpose,
Is the highest of calls.

So let us be grateful,
For every day we're here,
And cherish the moments,
That bring us joy and cheer.

For life is a blessing,
And it's up to us to make it great,
Through every trial and difficulty,
And with each step we take.

Celebrate yourself

Celebrate yourself, your amazing soul,
For all the times you've played your role,
In this crazy world we call our own,
You've stood up tall and have done it alone.

You've conquered fears and overcome doubt,
And chased dreams that once seemed far out,
You've spread love and light wherever you go,
And have never let your spirits get low.

You've laughed, you've cried, you've tripped over and fell,
But each time you rose and stood up so well,
You've learned, you've grown and you've become strong,
And with each new day, you sing a new song.

So celebrate yourself, for you are unique,
And there's no one out there who could ever assess,
The wonders you bring to this world each day,
You're a shining star, keep paving your way.

All I have is happiness

All I have is happiness,
It fills me up from within.
With every laugh and smile,
My spirit fly high, and I win.

There's sunshine in my heart,
And rainbows in my soul.
I'm grateful for the blessings,
That make me feel so whole.

I cherish each moment,
The good and the bad.
For I know that in the end,
I'll be glad for all I had.

Happiness is my treasure,
The one thing I hold.
And I'll hold onto it tightly,
With every beat of my chest.

For everything else may fade,
But happiness remains.
A constant source of joy,
That keeps me free from pains.

So I'll keep on smiling,
No matter what comes my way.
For all I have is happiness,
And it's here to stay.

You are far away

Oh, how I wish I could see you now,
To feel your touch and hear your sound,
But as we are miles apart,
We must learn to distance our work of art.

Our love does not confine,
To the walls of our office and room,
For it is the universe that binds,
Our hearts in a love that forever blooms.

Distance may be a challenge we embrace,
But this barrier shall not bring us to disgrace,
For every day, we choose to fight,
To keep our love strong and bright.

We may not be holding hands,
Or sharing the same sleep,
But our hearts are intertwined,
In a love so true and genuine.

For in this journey of loneliness,
We may find comfort and peace,
As we support our connection,
And keep the love alive, piece by piece.

So let distance be the test we shall overcome,
For our hearts are bound in a love that never comes undone,
And though the days may seem long and tough,
Our long distance love will always be enough.

Peace and healing as I travel

The open road invite me to roam,
To find peace and happiness, my own home.
For there's something special in traveling,
Away from the routine, so unappealing.

As I drive mile after mile,
My worries and fears start to smile.
The world becomes my playground,
And opportunities for adventure surround.

Every view and sound that I encounter,
There is a melody that fills me with wonder.
From towering peaks to deep blue seas,
In this beauty, I find eternal peace.

The air I breathe is pure and free,
A healing in my mind and body, I guarantee.
My spirit fly high, without a care,
On this journey, I find a peace of mind.

Every stop along the way,
Brings new people and sights to move slowly.
Connections made, friendships born,
In this nice life, we are beautiful.

For healing and joy go hand in hand,
And travel offers both.
A journey that nurtures our soul,
In its embrace, we find ourselves whole.

Sharing is caring

Sharing is caring,
It's what we should do,
To spread love and kindness,
And make hearts new.

When we share our thoughts,
Our feelings and dreams,
We open up ourselves,
To new possibilities it seems.

Sharing a love can be powerful,
It can touch someone's heart,
And bring joy to their day,
And set them on a new start.

So let's share our kindness,
With those near and far,
And let the power of lover,
Bring us closer than we are.

Growing up comes with a responsibility

Growing up comes with a responsibility,
To take charge and uphold the ability,
To make decisions and lead our own life,
To pave our own path and face every obstacle.

No more can we blame the world for our mistakes,
Or expect others to clean up after our snows,
For we are adults, mature and wise,
And must take control of our own actions.

We must learn to shoulder our own load,
To not give up and hit the road,
To face challenges and overcome fears,
To work hard and dry our own tears.

Growing up is a journey of growth and change,
Of learning new things and a wider range,
Of understanding others and our own selves,
Of taking responsibility and being true ourselves.

So let us embrace the responsibility that comes with age,
And not shy away from the hardships of the stage,
For growing up means facing the world head on,
And proving to ourselves that we are strong.

So much pain

The pain is too much,
My heart feels crushed,
Heavy burdens weighing me down,
Tears fall like rain, without a sound.

The world spins too fast,
Painful memories, really last,
I can't escape this suffering,
Fighting for strength, it's hard to see.

Every breath feels like a struggle,
Hopelessness, makes me buckle,
I pray for peace, for some relief,
But the pain, is a constant thief.

I try to stand up, to be strong,
But sometimes it's just too long,
The pain is too much to bear,
Wishing for someone, anyone to care.

Although the pain is too much,
I won't give up, I'll fight as such,
Taking one step at a time,
Hoping for the day, when I'll shine. .

It was mine and I let it go

It was mine, that precious thing,
But I let it slip away,
Like a bird that spread its wings,
And soared into the day.

It was mine, that passing dream,
But I didn't fight to keep,
But now it's gone, or so it seems,
And my heart is left to Shred tears.

I watched it go, with regret,
As it faded out of sight,
My chance, my love, my one regret,
Lost in the dark of night.

But though it's gone, I won't lose hope,
For life is full of new chances,
And though this loss is hard to bear,
My heart will find something true.

It was mine, that special thing,
But I let it go with grace,
And though it caused my heart to sing,
It's time to give another space.

Simplify your life

Life is not hard, my dear,
You just need to simplify it.
Clear the space and noise in your head,
And focus on the present instead.

Stop worrying about the future and past,
Live in this moment, make it last.
Find joy in the little things each day,
And let go of things that weigh.

Do what you love, love what you do,
Follow your heart, it will guide you through.
Embrace each challenge as a chance to grow,
And appreciate the beauty around you, let it show.

Life is not complicated, it's simple and free,
Just open your eyes, and you will see.
That happiness lies within your reach,
So embrace life with an open heart, and it will teach.

When the Dream is over

Dreams are fragile things, born in our heads,
Flitting through our minds like short lived organism,
Taking root in our consciousness, spreading their wings,
Growing and falling on the hope that they bring.

But all dreams must end, at least in this world,
Fading away, their precious success,
Leaving us to wonder where they have gone,
Leaving us to mourn their passing, alone.

The dream is over, its light is now extinguished,
Leaving us lost, feeling defeated,
But still we must go on, and still we must try,
To find new dreams to lift us to the sky.

For though this dream may now be gone,
Its message waitaround, can still live on,
A guiding light that shines within,
Pushing us forward, to begin again.

I will shower you with love

I will shower you with love,
Like drops of rain from up above.
I'll takeoff your thirst with tender care,
And turn your heart from hopelessness.

My love will flow like a river,
Overflowing with sweet effort.
I'll hold you close and never let go,
With each passing moment, my love will grow.

I'll kiss you gently on the cheek,
And whisper words of love unique.
I'll light up your world with a smile,
And walk with you every single mile.

I'll be your anchor in life's stormy sea,
And protect you from all misery.
My love for you will never fade,
For in your heart, my love is made.

So let me shower you with love,
From now until and ever.
I'll never stop loving you,
For in my heart, you're forever true.

The future is in our hands

The future is in our hands,
We hold the power to shape the land,
To make it brighter or to dim,
We must act now, and not give in.

It's up to us to do what's right,
To spread compassion, love, and light,
To develop a better place,
For all who share this wonderful space.

We must work together, hand in hand,
And build a future that is outstanding,
One where kindness rules the day,
Where peace and justice hold control.

The choices we make today,
Will shape the course of things to come,
So let us choose with care,
And make our future strong and bold.

Let's strive to dream and reach for the sky,
Let hope and courage guide our eyes,
For the future is in our hands,
The power to create is in our command.

Self-Esteem

I am worthy, I am strong,
I can do anything all day long.
My self-esteem is high and true,
I have confidence in all I do.

I am beautiful, inside and out,
I have no fear or doubt.
I am capable of achieving my dreams,
I am in control, so it seems.

I love myself, just as I am,
I don't need anyone's approval.
I am unique, there is no one like me,
I embrace my flaws and let them be.

I am grateful for all that I have,
I live life with joy and love.
I believe in myself, and that's overwhelming,
With my self-esteem, I stand my ground.

So, let the world see who I am,
With my self-esteem, I'll take a stand.
I am worthy, I am strong,
I can do anything all day long.

Your mind is your weapon

Your mind is your weapon,
A powerful tool indeed.
With it you can conquer mountains,
And fulfill your every need.

The thoughts you think are yours alone,
And shape the world you see.
So choose them wisely, carefully,
And let them set you free.

If negativity creeps in,
And tries to bring you down,
Remember that your mind is strong,
And turn your thoughts around.

With focus and determination,
And a positive attitude,
You can make your dreams a reality,
And achieve great levels.

So use your mind as your weapon,
And fight for what you believe.
With strength and courage in your heart,
You'll achieve all you conceive.

I hold this pen in my hand, writing poems

I.

love and pain,
words that flow like a gentle rain.

With each stroke of the pen,
I pour out my heart
onto the paper, a work of art.

In every line, I see myself,
a reflection of my dreams and hopes,
of the joys and sorrows that I've felt.

I write of love that's sweet and true,
of the bond that two hearts share,
of the trust and faith that they renew.

And when I write of pain and loss,
of broken hearts that bleed and weep,
my words become a bridge across.

For in these verses, you will find
a familiar echo of your own heart,
a solace for your troubled mind.

So I hold this pen in my hand,
writing poems for you to read,
a gift of beauty that I hope will stand.

II.

With each stroke of my pen,
I pour out my heart and soul,
Ink flowing freely like a river,
As new ideas and emotions take control.

I write of love and loss,
Of hope and despair,
Of the beauty of nature,
And the challenges we bear.

Each word I choose with care,
Crafting lines with precision,
For every poem I write,
Is a reflection of my vision.

And when I finish a creation,
I feel a sense of satisfaction,
For I have captured a moment,
In words of profound action.

So I continue to hold my pen,
Writing poems day and night,
For through poetry, I express myself,
And bring my innermost thoughts to light.

About the Author

Segapelo Samuel Kagiso is a multifaceted personality with diverse talents and accomplishments. Born and raised in Vrede, Rustenburg (South Africa) , he is a visionary entrepreneur, a passionate writer, and a believer in the power of words to inspire and motivate others.

Segapelo's journey towards entrepreneurship began with his fascination with technology. He pursued his passion by studying Diploma in Information Technology and worked as a Computer Engeneer before venturing out on his own. He own an IT company that provides cutting-edge IT solutions to businesses and organizations across South Africa.

Along with his work in the technology sector, Segapelo is also a gifted writer. He writes poetry and stories that inspire and uplift readers. He believes that words have the power to heal and transform lives, and his work reflects that belief. Segapelo's writing often explores themes of resilience, perseverance, and hope, encouraging readers to overcome challenges and pursue their dreams.

In addition to his entrepreneurial and creative pursuits, Segapelo is also a co-founder of a construction company that provides mining and industrial supplies to businesses in South Africa. Through his work, he has created job opportunities and contributed to the economic growth of his community.

About the book

Introducing "The hills that built me" - a collection of life-inspiring poems that will touch your heart and soul. This book is a reflection of the author's experiences, thoughts, and emotions throughout his and other's life journey.

Through this collection of poems, Segapelo invites readers to take a journey with 'him, exploring the highs and lows of life, the joys and sorrows, and the moments of inspiration that have helped shape his and other's perspective.

Each poem in " The hills that built me " is a window into the Author's heart is a reflection of the struggles and victories that have made them who they are today. From the pain of loss to the beauty of love, from the darkness of despair to the light of hope, these poems capture the essence of life in all its complexity.

Whether you're looking for inspiration, comfort, or simply a moment of reflection, "The hills that built me" has something for everyone. This book is a testament to the power of poetry to heal and uplift, to connect us to each other and to the world around us.

So take a journey with the author through the pages of " The hills that built me," and discover the beauty and magic of life through the lens of poetry.

9 780639 782799